THROUGH THEIR EYES

WORD WEAVERS

Edited By Jenni Harrison

First published in Great Britain in 2020 by:

Young Writers
Remus House
Coltsfoot Drive
Peterborough
PE2 9BF
Telephone: 01733 890066
Website: www.youngwriters.co.uk

All Rights Reserved
Book Design by Ashley Janson
© Copyright Contributors 2020
Softback ISBN 978-1-80015-080-5

Printed and bound in the UK by BookPrintingUK
Website: www.bookprintinguk.com
YB0451L

FOREWORD

Since 1991, here at Young Writers we have celebrated the awesome power of creative writing, especially in young adults, where it can serve as a vital method of expressing strong (and sometimes difficult) emotions, a conduit to develop empathy, and a safe, non-judgemental place to explore one's own place in the world. With every poem we see the effort and thought that each pupil published in this book has put into their work and by creating this anthology we hope to encourage them further with the ultimate goal of sparking a life-long love of writing.

Through Their Eyes challenged young writers to open their minds and pen bold, powerful poems from the points-of-view of any person or concept they could imagine – from celebrities and politicians to animals and inanimate objects, or even just to give us a glimpse of the world as they experience it. The result is this fierce collection of poetry that by turns questions injustice, imagines the innermost thoughts of influential figures or simply has fun.

The nature of the topic means that contentious or controversial figures may have been chosen as the narrators, and as such some poems may contain views or thoughts that, although may represent those of the person being written about, by no means reflect the opinions or feelings of either the author or us here at Young Writers.

We encourage young writers to express themselves and address subjects that matter to them, which sometimes means writing about sensitive or difficult topics. If you have been affected by any issues raised in this book, details on where to find help can be found at *www.youngwriters.co.uk/info/other/contact-lines*

CONTENTS

Abbey Community College, Monkstown

Josh McClinton (14)	1
Katie Smyth (13)	2
Alex Robinson	4
Jake Bingham	5
Kara Logan	6
Evie McClintock	7
Ross Thompson (13)	8

Alcester Grammar School, Alcester

Oreoluwa Kikiowo (13)	9
Alice Rose Battersby (14)	10

Bartley Green School, Bartley Green

Keira Morgan	12
Ethan Coley (13)	14
Tilly Large (12)	15
Kyra Sahdra	16
Zhane Smith (12)	17
Mckiah Noormohamed (12)	18
Charmaine Makunde (11)	20
Trinity West	21
Aqdas Merchant	22
Eve Hilton	23

Clayfields House, Stapleford

Roman Ilyas (15)	24
Jodie Billingham (14)	25
Niki Evans (16)	26

Redmaids' High School, Westbury On Trym

Louise Lord (14)	27
Anna Wielenga (15)	28
Poppy Trower (14)	30
Peggy Barnes (14)	32

Simon Langton Girls' Grammar School, Canterbury

Emma Ralph (13)	33
Alice Higgins (13)	34
Gemma Small (13)	36
Rhiannon Jaynes (13)	38
Juliette Messenger (13)	40
Maisie Illman (13)	42
Kesia Kuriakose (14)	44
Alice Starr (13)	46
Felicity Browning (12)	48
Madeleine Spencer (13)	50
Daisy Alexander-Bailey (12)	52
Zoe Adams Waldstein (12)	53
Phoebe Payne (12)	54
River Palmer (12)	56
Ebony Ferguson (13)	58
Eliza Geering (13)	60
Lily Barnes (13)	62
Lucy Watson (13)	64
Bethan McClean (14)	65
Katherine Lindsay (13)	66
Leila Duddy (13)	68
Orissa Barrett (12)	69
Maja Dembska (12)	70
Skye Thomson (12)	71
Lola Hewson (13)	72

Duwari Giridharan (12)	74
Martha Clegg (12)	75
Laila Giles (12)	76
Emma Deery (12)	78
Luella-Mai Watson (13)	80
Tia Anto (12)	82
Iris Hill (14)	83
Claudia Carlotti (13)	84
Amy Rowland (12)	85
Isla O'Leary (12)	86
Emily Crooks (13)	87
Amelia Green (13)	88
Athena Martin (12)	89
Aoife Mullaney (13)	90
Eve Horsfield-Burke (13)	91
Anna Murray (13)	92
Luisa Williams (12)	93
Aania Rehman (12)	94
Marwa Hassan (12)	95
Josephine O'Sullivan (13)	96
Summer Hamilton (12)	97
Annie Boyson (12)	98
Hannah Oven (13)	99
Alexa Steadwood (13)	100
Charlotte Rawlins (12)	101
Elsa Busuttil (13)	102
Lily Herron-Jones (12)	104
Esmé Thompsett (12)	105
Sophie Crane (12)	106
Miriam Thorpe (12)	107
Rosie Taborn (13)	108
Ella-Mai Rodwell (13)	109

Walney School, Walney

Phoebe Lovidge (14)	110

Westborough High School, Dewsbury

Amna Ramzan (12)	111
Libby Williams (14)	112

Wirral Grammar School For Girls, Bebington

Rowan Abass (13)	113

THE
POEMS

Death Row

When I sleep I dream of the electric chair.
What will happen to me I pray, as I am unaware.
Will they put me in this contraption?
With an audience watching like a carnival attraction!
Will it be painful? Will they cheer?
Or will it be calm while they all peer?

Will one day the truth come out?
Where people realise what I am truly about!
I didn't murder that man that day?
I found him still and stopped to pray!
I'm an innocent man with clean hands of this crime,
Yet all I have now is a limited time!

When the time comes Lord please take my soul,
Don't leave me behind and out in the cold,
I pray you hear me, I pray you do,
I beg for a miracle to come true.
Should I be spared or should I not?
I only wish not to be forgot.
Love each other and hold them dear,
For we never know when the end is near.

Josh McClinton (14)
Abbey Community College, Monkstown

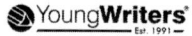

Bullying

As I approached my new school,
I was sweating, I needed water to cool.
My anxiety went very high,
"Oh my! Look at the time."
I felt so uncomfortable and went to class,
First period I had maths.
I knew I was going to have an awful year,
Getting bullied is my number one fear.

Next day, I smiled and walked in,
The bullying was about to begin.
Two girls walked up to me,
Hurting me and making fun of me.
I dashed down the hallway.
Crying with tears,
That I'm going through my fear.
Why does everyone hate me?
This wasn't what I thought it would be.
Why should I change for them?
I'll never be like them.
I'm afraid to tell anyone about this,
As I will get punched by a fist.
I don't know if hiding is right,
As I have lost all my might.
I would be paying the price,
Being walked over and trapped like mice.
Why can't they be nice?

Never change who you are,
As bullying would go too far.
Everyone is different in their own ways,
Every child deserves to play.
Be the person you are,
As we stop bullying going too far.
Face our fears,
As bullying needs to be clear.
Talk to someone who you trust,
Don't lie there in the dust.

Katie Smyth (13)
Abbey Community College, Monkstown

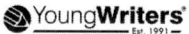

Ode To Theresa May

Oh Theresa May, I'm writing to say
How I think you're better than they.
For they say, "You weren't great",
But I say horse... faeces.

And even though they made fun of you,
I still think you're great,
And oh yes, your dancing was stoic.
But no, it was not your fault

And I hope you know that I do blame a few
And none of them are you:
Corbyns, Camerons and Johnsons.

And I admire your speech and I do believe that
You're truly one of the greats,
And to quote you "Second female Prime Minister
and definitely not the last."

Alex Robinson
Abbey Community College, Monkstown

Flying High

I've loved the sky ever since I was a little boy.
I wanted to dance in the sky, bounce from cloud to cloud
and have fun in the sun.
But now, I'm up here shooting guns.
Every one swerving inside and out...
My engine fails, the last spark goes out!

I'm now swooshing and swerving
In the sky my thoughts in my head
Am I going to die?
Smoke is blocking the windows
I take out my picture of my wife.
Don't even know if I will lose my life.
I wish there was no war. Not even
A single fight if I could I would change
It with all my might.

Jake Bingham
Abbey Community College, Monkstown

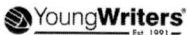

A Soldier's Life

My heart's in the right place
But I want to go home
Nowhere to weep, nowhere to roam
But all I want to do is go home.

Bombs going off, nowhere to go
I'm showing the people a brave show.
Doing this for my country, I do not feel safe,
I just want my heart in the right place.

Most of our soldiers are missing home,
But with guns to our chest
And bombs to our homes.
We might not make it safely back home.

Day to day, night to night
I suffered my body just to fight.

Kara Logan
Abbey Community College, Monkstown

There Is Always A Light

I cry myself to sleep at night,
Just wishing it would stop
Maybe tomorrow it will decrease
Then maybe, it might not

I'm sorry I don't impress you,
Don't act the way you want
I'm sorry I'm not pretty
And don't have much to flaunt

They mock me as I sit here,
They mock me in my sleep
It goes on and on every day
Another piece of me is chiselled away

When you feel that you are in the dark,
There will always be a light
There are people who are there for you
To ask 'are you alright'.

Evie McClintock
Abbey Community College, Monkstown

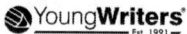

Alcatraz

Sirens flashing red and blue
Bags full of green, dream come true
Police surrounding like a pack of wolves
Guns blazing, bullets flying, bodies dropping
Hands cuffed, wrists cramped
Speed boating, wind blowing
Spoon shanks, psychopaths wielding knifes
Foggy night, is no sight
As well as a stormy night
In the morning people moaning.

Ross Thompson (13)
Abbey Community College, Monkstown

Internet Getaway

I read, I study, I learn every day
What can I do? Can life be dull and grey?
When evening comes, after my shift at the cafe
The blue light calls my name
I open my laptop and make the world go away

I can be whoever I want to be
A model, an actress, even have a degree
In my bed, in my PJs
I become a pilot travelling the world
Making friends as I go along
I live in a mansion, with a pet and cat poodle
Eating a fancy dinner each night, at least not noodles
I'm a new person, living a lie
Morning has come and I must say goodbye

This might be an old cliché
But behind the screen is my resting place
On the Internet getaway.

Oreoluwa Kikiowo (13)
Alcester Grammar School, Alcester

Pankhurst

Breaking news! Breaking news!
Igniting a spark
To blaze and to burn
Creating the new

A woman of vision
Of progress, not thought
To lead us to Heaven
Or lead us
To naught.

Is she a terrorist
Her with eyes of blackened storm
Her with broken, cracked skin
Shards strewn over the pavement
Like searing glass
And abandoned now, when
Someone cries full of fight
"Curse those blasted women!"
But solitary, forlorn?

Is she a heroine?
Her with voice of strength saturate
Her with will of hidden hope
And hands audacious enough
To grip nations of women

Fixated and eager
Their eyes bound to her
In bondage of freedom?

I know not. I am
A mere woman, unprepared
Untrained
Hardly a soldier
Not yet
But
Ready for orders

Like sparrow
Flocking with eagle
Terrorist heroine
General.

Alice Rose Battersby (14)
Alcester Grammar School, Alcester

Dance

Dance is the blood, sweat and tears
from a tough session.
Dance is the feeling of
"You can't do this."
Dance is thinking to yourself
that you're never going to be as good as her.
Dance is failing and failing
time and time again.
Dance is the pain you go through
every time.

Dance is coming out of your shell
and building that confidence you need in life.
Dance is letting go of everything,
when you have had a bad day at school.
Dance is expressing your thoughts
through music and movements.
Dance is not holding back,
with not a care in the world.
Dance is the feeling of having no limits,
that anything is possible.
Dance is carrying on,
when you thought you couldn't do it anymore.

Dance is getting back up again
when you fall.
Dance is not being able to do everything
that you should be able to do.
Dance is the stress
that you think you might forget your routine.

Dance is everything.
Dance is life.
So never give up
because you are special,
you are amazing.

Keira Morgan
Bartley Green School, Bartley Green

What Is It Like Having A Mental Illness?

What's going on in people's heads?
Is it gaming, writing, or wishing to go to bed?
Some people might not have a 'normal' brain
From the inside it can cause them lots of pain.

Depression, anxiety, addiction - there's a wide range
People question them, "Why do they act 'strange'?"
Not thinking straight, all of the others
If you think about it, who does it really bother?

Thoughts that are lonely, and scary and bleak
The ones inside of you that can make your heart break.
Don't let it get big, keep it in order
You don't want to feel its weight on your shoulders.

Now what about people with a horrible past?
If you lived their stories, then you might not last
PTSD and trauma are what it's known as
Don't let anything scar you, just let it all pass.

If you have any of these, or think that you do
Be sure to ask someone, they can help you.
Don't let it rise and make you drown
If you can open up it'll truly help to make it stop.

Ethan Coley (13)
Bartley Green School, Bartley Green

Losing Myself: In Plain Sight

There is a sadness inside that won't go away,
Although it's not welcome, it chooses to stay.
It's buried itself inside, really deep.
Now it is my burden, to carry and keep.

It's been so long since I can remember a time,
Where the thoughts in my head were actually mine.
I tried to find the light, yet the darkness pulls me in,
I try to find the calm, but there's just chaos within.

I'm overwhelmed by the pressure to make things just right,
But I don't think they have it in them to see what's in sight.
The pain I carry inside, they don't have a clue,
They clearly have no idea, just what I'm going through.
The turmoil I hold, they think they can relate,
They never really will, until it may be too late.

I'm drifting away, it's so draining each day,
I hope for the strength to keep this heartache at bay,
Until I am able to climb out of this hole
That swallows me away.

Tilly Large (12)
Bartley Green School, Bartley Green

Suffering

She walks the halls, her head down low
Tries her hardest not to be seen,
But I know what's going on,
I see the way her thoughts have been.

She says, "I'm fine" and "I'm okay"
It's ironic, isn't it, what we all say?
It's on her face, it's in her eyes,
I see it! No make-up can disguise.

The scars on her wrist, are they helping?
Her head has definitely stopped spinning,
Within minutes, feeling the world is ending
Another scratch, excuse, lie, tear
They don't understand why you can no longer bear!

Everyone's got something bottled up inside,
Try to drown it but it just seems to survive.
If she would have talked, then she would've realised,
She's beautiful, smart and could achieve it all
She viewed her future to be, since aged five.

Kyra Sahdra
Bartley Green School, Bartley Green

Earth

What is it?
Is it a circle of blue?
Or is it a clue
to teach us just
how to live through and through?

Is it how the sky flies high?
Or how you sit next to the calm blue sea?
Is it how the sand crunches under your feet?
Or how the wind whispers softly?
Is it how the grass swings,
while the birds start to sing?

Isn't it when all is said and done
the Earth, at our hands, turns to crumbs?
When factories start to burn
and the Earth starts to turn
quicker and quicker to slush
our existence into mush.

As we start to fade away,
the Earth will no longer play
with its friends up in space.
So listen to me now,
If you want to stay, we must change.
If we don't,
we will lose our children's beloved home!

Zhane Smith (12)
Bartley Green School, Bartley Green

Racism

Racism
Quite a gigantic problem
Not quite everybody believes
Everyone is equal
Prejudice held against people's race
This should not be the case.

Some believe your race
Determines who you are
This should not be the case.
Everyone is equal; has equal rights.

Imagine,
An oak and a willow, two trees
No difference other than their leaves
Surely you would agree
Both are trees
As equal to each other,
Colour doesn't matter -
It doesn't change what's underneath.

After all,
We didn't get the chance to choose to be short
Or tall, neither did we get to choose
The colour of our skin.

Now you have heard,
Stop and think
If you see any racism
Stop it within a blink.

Mckiah Noormohamed (12)
Bartley Green School, Bartley Green

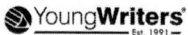

Follow Your Future

Remember
Every day, follow your own rhythm
Be honest to yourself, don't keep yourself hidden
Express innate beauty, what feels most natural
It's your true beauty, that's truly admirable.

Live a life that aligns all your beliefs,
Not one that only pleases elites
Don't confirm just to conform
Follow your future to positively transform.

Choice is a gift that we were all given,
Embrace it each day and live your vision.
Find your worth which shines just when you do
When no external gain will give that to you.

You have deep within, a very special flow
Follow that and I promise you will certainly glow.
Find your true nature, by listening to your heart,
Live true to yourself and become living art.

Charmaine Makunde (11)
Bartley Green School, Bartley Green

Imagination

As humans we reach
for a world beyond our own
We climb and clamber away
from Nature's zone.
We get sucked in
to our imagination
- colours swirling free.
Our minds make pictures
of new things that we see.

We don't have to be lonely
to reach depths of creation.
If we put our minds to it
we'll find us pure elation.
There's nothing that can stop us,
we can run rogue, run free.
Our minds make stories
of new things that we see.

We can pour it out on paper,
not choose to share at all
it's yours and your choice only
let it out and let it free.
Our minds make paintings
of new things that we see.

Trinity West
Bartley Green School, Bartley Green

Badminton

Starts off with just a hit,
becomes a violent competition,
everyone is engaged,
not knowing the outcome.
Heads go back and forth
from court to court.
Players to players
still no clue on the outcome.
Anything can change
at any time.

The flick of the wrist can change everything
the way that you hit it
how you hit it
changes the whole game.

The anger that builds,
what will it make them do? Don't know.
What are they thinking? Don't know.
Will they hit or will they miss? Don't know.
You will never know, never.

Aqdas Merchant
Bartley Green School, Bartley Green

The Crow

It swoops down low
The direction the wind blows.

Perches on the lamp post
Glaring at the beach's coast.

The sadness it'll bring
From its tail to its wing.

Some call it deathly
Treated so unfairly.

Recognisable by its feathers
It sweeps away harsh weather.

Although the crow is the loneliest
It could be quite the friendliest.

Never judge what you don't know
You never know the lengths you'll go.

Eve Hilton
Bartley Green School, Bartley Green

I Am A House

I am a house
And people live inside of me
But I do not appreciate them
Because they do not appreciate me

They throw their dirty socks on the floor
I just can't take it anymore

The family continues to increase
One baby, two baby, three baby, four
Extreme mess and very noisy
Their nappies stink
Under the sink

My garden is full of weeds and dog poop
No matter what I do, the fiends don't scoop
Not to mention the dog's constant bark
They never take it to the park

The deafening drone of the washing machine
Nothing is as it seems
Except for at night when they're all asleep
And each of their dreams I keep.

Roman Ilyas (15)
Clayfields House, Stapleford

Homeless

Once older
Everything gets colder
A rock-bottom floor
Is where I found myself poor
I wish there was a better law
I'm so weak I can hardly speak
Listening to my belly grumble
Help me please I mumble
People call me an old hag
Because all I wear is a rag
And carry an old carrier bag
My back aches
My heart breaks
Sitting there begging with my empty cup
Hoping there's a little bit of luck
I'm getting toward sixty
Getting a bit misty
No one needs me
I lost my family
Hoping God will one day take me away
That I'll be born again.

Jodie Billingham (14)
Clayfields House, Stapleford

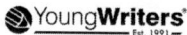

Mum

I miss my daughter
We are currently far apart
But connected by heart

The years of worry I have had
Now the worry is over I'm glad

I sleep at night knowing my daughter
Is safe and sober
My worries are finally over

Now I have a more healthy heart
The family won't fall apart

Our youngest boy is a pure joy
The love we share cannot be compared

Mother the kids from the start
Best friends forever from the heart.

Niki Evans (16)
Clayfields House, Stapleford

Home

My silky soft flippers scratch away,
All my energy goes into this one push,
To escape my spherical prison...
Free. No mother waits for me.

I amble along coarse gravel
Rubbing against my glossy casing,
A glowing crescent appears in the heavens
The bath of God's salty tears remains restless.

Roaring beasts charge towards me
Their luminous eyes light the way in all directions,
Glaring lamps gleam from static structures.
Which way do I go?

Dark monstrous shapes creep closer
Their prolonged pincers ready to pounce,
No stars shine to light the way
My necessity grows to find the hostile sea.

My chances are few,
Submerging myself in temperate waters
And sampling seaweed
Is only a dream for some.

Louise Lord (14)
Redmaids' High School, Westbury On Trym

Your Prey

I am lying on a shelf,
Cold.
Milk stares at me, says, "You're next."
Steps.
The door traps me in.
I can't escape the cold -
Or you.

The door bursts open,
Turning the spotlight on above me.
Your hand reaches,
Strangles me,
Lifts me from the shelf,
Then places me on plastic.
You make for the fridge once more,
To strangle more of my kind.

Your massive hand grabs a blade,
Slices through my orange flesh.
Removes my leafy hair.
The blade moves quick -
Quicker down my body.
Shoves me
- Or what is left of me -
Into boiling water.

I am sliced apart.
I am boiled alive.
I am brutally killed.
I don't want to die.
Not now.
Not ever.
I don't want to be
Your prey.

Anna Wielenga (15)
Redmaids' High School, Westbury On Trym

Faceless

Right, left, right, left
I march
In heavy boots that mangle feet
Dragging my rifle

Right, left, right, left
I march
As comrades fall on the pock-marked
Earth of the battlefield

Right, left, right, left
I march
With photographs pressed to my heart
Still beating - for now

Right, left, right, left
I march
Uniform wet with dark red rain
Bullets whistling past

Right, left, right, left
I march
Fighting a war I did not start
Maiming and killing

Right, left, right, left
I march
And I just
Keep
On marching

Until morning.

Poppy Trower (14)
Redmaids' High School, Westbury On Trym

Burning Truth

My life is on fire
How do I know?
I am just a koala
My standards are low

I see you humans
Posting 'online'
"Australia Ablaze!"
And how we are dying

But what will that do?
It won't give us rain
Won't banish the fires
We still feel the pain

But what do I know?
I'm just a koala
But I can still feel
And this is a disaster.

Peggy Barnes (14)
Redmaids' High School, Westbury On Trym

Destruction

Right in the morning these evil things arrive
Straight into the forest, like sharks they dive
They chop down trees as if it's all for fun
Yet little do they know, what damage it has done

Every day they come with the saw
Taking the wood away just for a door
And each time I ask my monkey self
Is this doing any good to their health?

It isn't just me they do this thing to
I see other chimps dying through you
Sometimes I ask myself when will this stop?
Probably when the forest is full of new shops

I'm getting so cross as well as the trees
But still they take them away within a breeze
You wouldn't like it the other way round
When they come all at once, it's like the dog pound

It has gone on forever
They think it's so clever
But what they don't get
Is how I'm on my last legs

Maybe in the future they'll change their minds
Before all is gone in my monkey kind
No I'm sure they won't they all find it fun
So I think unless I want to die, we all must run!

Emma Ralph (13)
Simon Langton Girls' Grammar School, Canterbury

Is This Me?

Help! I want to scream but can't
Twisted in every way, what is happening?
I'm bursting with emotions, is this me?
Stop! I don't think I belong here, why do I need to fit in?
Because I'm judged constantly
Eyes glaring right through my soul
Then the rumours and whispers run and soar
Through the winds. Is this me?

Why! Why am I seeing this?
Text after text
'Fat', 'ugly', 'not good enough',
When will the torment end?
Tearing my mind in two
Stay true to myself or they are right
I should change, is this me?

Please! Please stop
My bruises are bad enough as it is
Don't pin me against the wall
And glare at me with those dragon eyes, you monster
I can't ask for help as my voice is lost
In a sea of waves, is this me?

Huff! This test is so hard
Why did I get the grade I got?
I'm stupid and everyone is better than me
I should just shrivel up and die

Rot, sink through the floor
What does it matter
I'm dead when people find out my grades anyway
As As turn to Ds, is this me?

No! I can't do this anymore
I feel so different, a stranger to myself
What happened, why am I so lost?
In the dark all on my own
No one to hold me up from falling deep
Into the monstrous pit of school, social media,
People, friends, bullying, grades
Trying to fit in and identify
People go through this every day
Voices lost in sounds
Nothing is done
Or is it just a phase in life
Everyone goes through? Is this me?

Listen! This is today's society,
We can't help it, we can't stop it
They make us feel like we want to leave
And get out of here
We can try to tame it, not let it affect us
Or we will crash and burn in our lost thoughts
Of fury and sadness.
I am me!

Alice Higgins (13)
Simon Langton Girls' Grammar School, Canterbury

There Is Always A Choice

Summer's over and so am I
I gave up all I had
I finally saw things eye to eye
I was done making everyone and even myself mad

I walk into the zoo full of hungry beasts
Ready to pick on all their prey
Before they start their many feasts
Oh god, it's time to start the day!

Walking through the hall
Alone
I'm now seen as small
Wishing I was unknown

It feels like I'm not where I'm meant to be
I don't fit in with all these familiar faces
But I'm finally free
I'm filling in those missing spaces

I wish I could go back and change the past
Be a little braver and stood up for what's right
I wish I never let it last
I thought I could see dark and light

I couldn't stop dreaming that I could be someone different
More than a stupid and mean high school girl
I look around and start to give out a compliment
Then I stopped my whirl

I no longer thought I'd said too much
My mind and heart felt steady
I no longer needed my crutch
I was ready!

I still miss those days
When I was young and naive
When the only stress was following the craze
I wish I never had to leave

Six months later
I'm happy and content
No longer the dream breaker
I threw away all my years of torment

I crave a smile
I'm no longer fragile
No need to judge an online profile
Or anyone's style

Let's stand together
Don't be the one to ignite the fire
Make this message last forever
And remember you're never alone so inspire
Stop bullying!

Gemma Small (13)
Simon Langton Girls' Grammar School, Canterbury

The Shadow Man

There was a voice
That I didn't want to hear by choice
All alone I tried to fight it
But no one could stop him

He was my shadow
I was his prey
Waiting, watching,
Ready to pounce
But no one could stop him

They see me as strange,
Stranger, strangest
I'm a mad hatter
Enclosed in the walls of this madhouse
He trapped me here
I'm a secret in a safe
But no one could stop him

As every tear from the clouds hit my pillow
He got closer
The whispers became voices
The voices became shouts
But no one could stop him

Breathless I pant
My head crowded like the agitated pills in my case
A drip from a tap

Seeking attention
Water in a glass; still and settled
Unlike me

'Schizophrenia' they said
'Mentally unstable' they thought
For they couldn't hear his hush in the silence
They couldn't feel the chilling air as he drew closer
But no one could stop him

Alone... silent
The calm before the storm
As the darkness crept closer effortlessly
Surrounding me before his arrival
The door squealed in fear as he appeared
A tall, mysterious yet familiar figure
But no one could stop him

He stood there
Still as my eyes fixed upon him
His empty and solemn stare engulfed me
His soulless whispers drowned my thoughts
Paralysed in shock
Paralysed in fear
I sleep once more.

Rhiannon Jaynes (13)
Simon Langton Girls' Grammar School, Canterbury

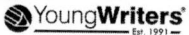

Create, Don't Hate!

I watch her cry
Endlessly, endlessly,
From the hate she gets
I sit there with sympathy

She might be a liar
And only eleven
But I honestly think
She could pretend she's seven

She wants to be older
Than she really is
Thirteen isn't her real age
Yet she says it is

Her mumma lies too
Nearly spilling the beans
She talks to the audience
On the live that she streams

With millions watching
From the other side
Their phones share out
The words that she cries

The hate comes through
From the comment section
Why hasn't she blocked it yet?
She never gets any love or affection

Only half her body is covered
None of her clothes are from Justice
As everyone tells her to shop there
Those people remain anonymous

I sit there on the side
As a blogging camera
But once her videos are done
My use is also over

I do still watch her
Through my lens
Yet she doesn't know it
I see her smile bend

She reads them out
Comment by comment
Gradually tearing
They become more extravagant

It happens every day
So she is used to it
But no one should be hurt
Like this did

If you're a hater
Then stop now
Go to the Queen Danielle
And bow.

Juliette Messenger (13)
Simon Langton Girls' Grammar School, Canterbury

The Mirror

I am the nettle amongst these flowers
The caterpillar amongst these butterflies
They are staring at me, I can tell
I'm not good enough.

I look in the mirror
I see a complete stranger looking back at me
I long for the days where it was simple
I'm not good enough.

I look again
I see an imperfect, worthless person looking right back at me
But this time, she's more familiar
Am I good enough?

Wait, something has changed
I now see a weak and vulnerable victim
Being forced into a certain lifestyle
Am I good enough?

A lifestyle full of pressure to be perfect
Will I ever escape?
I feel as if I am currently in a civil war, constantly fighting with myself
I'm not good enough.

I feel as though I am watching my life from the passenger's seat
Each day becoming slower and more tedious than the last
I'm not good enough

I look again, this time trying to disregard my feeling
Of destruction and isolation that was once a feeling of innocence
And confidence
Something's different

I look in the mirror
I see a girl
A girl who is broadminded to others, though not to herself
Am I good enough?

I look in the mirror one last time
I look straight into the girl's eyes, say
I am good enough.

Maisie Illman (13)
Simon Langton Girls' Grammar School, Canterbury

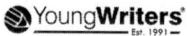

Bird's Eye View

Let's go back
As a creature soaring through the sky
Let's go back
Just one century back

Was our planet this ungrateful?

Such healthy green grass
Millions of life-giving trees
Water as clean as crystals
Animals hopping and springing about
The true beauty of nature and wildlife

Now let's travel back to the present

Not a single patch of grass without junk
Not one stream of water without plastic
Not one species without a threat
Oceans are perishing from mankind's selfishness
Was our planet really this ungrateful?

There's litter all around us
There's litter on the street
There's litter in the bushes
There's litter at your feet

Just see how much it cost
For our forests to turn from lots into lost

How much did you lose
Apart from those lush views?

Only after the last tree has been cut down
Only after the last river has been poisoned
Only after the last fish has been caught
Only then will you realise that money cannot be eaten

But always remember
That you can change
Before it changes you
You can make a difference.

Kesia Kuriakose (14)
Simon Langton Girls' Grammar School, Canterbury

The Boy In The Photograph

There is a boy in the photograph
That sits on the wall
I remember that boy
I remember him well

He used to hate the other boys in his class
They made him feel alien
They'd laugh at his long hair
And the way he wore a skirt

He would braid his friends' hair
And wear pink on his shirt
He loved pink
It was his favourite colour

When he went to visit Aunt Helen
She told him how much he'd grown
How much he'd blossomed
Blossomed into a gentleman

But being called a gentleman didn't seem right
The person in his head said no
Actually
The person in his head had a lot to say

They said he was a monster
They said he was an alien
But the person in his head could be kind too

They also wanted him to wear his sister's dresses
And put on his mother's make-up

There is a boy in the photograph
That sits on the wall
I know that boy, I know him well

She is no longer an alien
She is no longer a monster
She is no longer the boy in the photograph.

Alice Starr (13)
Simon Langton Girls' Grammar School, Canterbury

Trapped In A Bubble

Two friends sat together
All alone forever and ever
At least that's what they thought

They were soon torn apart
Even though they've been together
From the start

A new friend joined the pair
She added a new flair
Alas this wasn't to last

The two were always so close
They did everything together
Now their world was changing
Maybe it wasn't forever...

One friend missed the pair,
She thought that life wasn't fair
Although the other was oblivious and
Seemed not to care.

What was she to do?
It was tearing her apart
With every day that passed
She could feel it in her heart

She reminisced about the good times
All the fun summers that they'd had
Perhaps they'd all get back on track
And it wouldn't be as bad

I guess it just wasn't to be
The distance between them grew
There was nothing more to say
They were back to being a two
But it wasn't the pair from the start
One had a broken heart...

Felicity Browning (12)
Simon Langton Girls' Grammar School, Canterbury

The Ice Is Melting

The ice is melting
Earlier and earlier
Each year
I lose some of my home
Seals swim away like currents
In the sea
I can't catch them
They are only vulnerable
On the ice
No seals means no food
Not enough, not enough
For me, hungry as a whale
The cubs are starving too
We have done nothing wrong
Yet the humans do this
Climate change

The ice is melting
Earlier and earlier
Each year
I lose some of my home
Majestic, wild and free
Is how polar bears should live
Not vulnerable, a blue sheep
As we have become
The Earth calls for help
Yet I must save myself

A single polar bear
I cannot help
Around the world
Climate change is happening
Only humans can stop it

The ice is melting
Earlier and earlier
Each year
I lose some of my home
No animal can stop it
Only humans can help
Please save the polar bears
It's not too late

The ice is melting
But for this planet
There is still hope.

Madeleine Spencer (13)
Simon Langton Girls' Grammar School, Canterbury

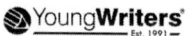

Plastic Pollution

Staring into the mid-sea blue,
I look beyond the coral to see you.
A weird flapping thing floating in mid-air,
with airless wings a bit like hair.
Next to you I see a shoal of fish,
swimming into thousands of hollow, shiny sticks.
Straws, say 'humans' on the ground,
they are the most 'dangerous animal' that is around!

Distorting our landscape, our habitat, the unknown
but what they don't know is they're destroying their own home!
In the eyes of what I see,
85% of our oxygen is produced right from the sea!
So if it wasn't for us to keep it clean,
you would barely have a chance to breathe, so why be so mean?

The next time in your life you see plastic,
think how much it's not fantastic!
The sea, the trees, the air, your ground
you better sort it out while we're still around!
So the next time you see some plastic near...
think about what you can change this year.
You need to reduce litter before we all drown,
you better not let us all down!

Daisy Alexander-Bailey (12)
Simon Langton Girls' Grammar School, Canterbury

The Future

'History will be kind to me for I intend to write it'
These are the words I live by
My hands will shape our future
I will mould it like clay
Bound to obey my every command

My eyes are the ones turned towards innovation
My voice is the one strong enough to command our soldiers
Strong enough to lead them into battle
And I am able to watch them fall in the name of advancement

This world will know my name
The name that will be carved into every scrap of metal shipped from my factories
The name that will give those scraps of metal life

I will tower above the cities on my throne of severed hands
And look upon the world I have created
The world that I can destroy with the wave of my hand
The screams of those below me echoing through my factory walls
The bodies of the weak will be the foundation of the future.

Zoe Adams Waldstein (12)
Simon Langton Girls' Grammar School, Canterbury

Why Is This Happening To Me?

Hard eyes capture mine once again
A sly smirk spreads across their malicious lips
Their sturdy grasp as strong as ever
Clutching onto my transfixed body
"Why is this happening to me?"

Punch after punch is delivered to my face
Causing blood to trickle down from my now split lip
Thick like honey
My blood is a scarlet river
Vulnerability overwhelms me
"Why is this happening to me?"

My raspy voice catches in my throat
I fight back the eager tears that are threatening to run free
All to be heard are our hitched breaths
"Why is this happening to me?"

I retrace the bruises
With an alarming touch
Pain sears through my body
Feeling as if I have been set aflame
"Why is this happening to me?"

I keep quiet
Praying that all of this will come to an end
Covering up my many scars

So that nobody will find out
"Why is this happening to me?"

Deathly silence replaces my last breath.

Phoebe Payne (12)
Simon Langton Girls' Grammar School, Canterbury

They Are Coming

My eyes flutter open
My head is pounding
My ears are ringing
Thoughts spiral through my mind
Where am I?
Why am I here?
Did I crash?
Or was I... taken?

The storms are irate
They assault the sky with candle flames
Burning the ground violently
They pass through it hastily
I lie still, the ground grumbles
It trembles through my body
It goes on and on...

No! It's not the storm
It's not an earthquake
It's footsteps of thousands
But maybe not human
They are coming
Coming closer
And closer.

I push myself up
I see them in the distance
My TARDIS dishevelled
Broken next to me
No escape, they keep coming
My pain struck me down
Like a spear through me.

They are here now
Metres away
I feel my eyelids getting heavier
I can't fight them...
Black, all I see is black
I am the Doctor, who are they?
They are the unknown.

River Palmer (12)
Simon Langton Girls' Grammar School, Canterbury

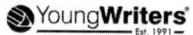

They Want A Normal Life

They are refugees
The ones who are terrorists
The ones who cause pain and despair
They aren't humans
They don't have emotions

They are refugees
The ones who are a threat
They should stay in their own country
They don't want peace
They don't know peace

They are refugees
The ones who fight
They fight for their lives
Why do they fight?
They shouldn't fight

They are refugees
The ones who need
Homes and a life again
The ones who cry from their loss
The ones who feel isolated

They are refugees
Who need support
They want peace

They don't want to fight
They fight for their lives

They aren't just refugees
They are humans
Lost in suffering
Trying to escape
They want their life back

They are children
And adults
Like everyone
They had a normal life
They want a normal life.

Ebony Ferguson (13)
Simon Langton Girls' Grammar School, Canterbury

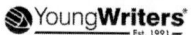

Now There Is No Orange Left Within The Sky

The camera took a shot
My face glistening like the sun
On the salty sea
No worries, no cover or camouflage, just me.

I was a flamingo in a flock of pigeons
All gathering to take a look
With my natural beauty
I was a princess in a book
And so the sun sat proudly
High in the sky.

Then a few years on my face turned slowly
Into a golden-brown lawn
And though I watered it every day
My face now had to be drawn.

I battled against the sand dunes
That now blew over my face
But still the clock went running
And it always won the race
Now the sun hung desperately
Low in the sky.

My younger sister came over last night
As I stared into the grimy glass
Now I sit with a shell of dust
To show the years that passed.

I'm now an unplayed violin
And the mirror that she bought
Is nothing more than the grimy glass
That carried away my thoughts.

Eliza Geering (13)
Simon Langton Girls' Grammar School, Canterbury

Emotions

Inside the mind
Lurking, ready to shout
Is a protester

Is that right?
Inside the mind
Sitting silently
Is a victim

That is still not right
Inside, listening to every word
Is a therapist

Are words no more
Then a rocky, rocking roller coaster
Inside my mind
Isolated in the corner
Is a prisoner

Someone help me
Inside, blocking every glimpse of light
A bully
I saw nothing

No words can help me now
Just in my head
Lost in my emotions
Is a teenager that looks like me

One word for you
Inside my mind
Their face so gleeful
Their eyes start to see the light
Is a teenager who looks like your best friend too

I embrace myself
Be positive, I think
Be happy and grin like a Cheshire cat

The teenager's hushed thoughts sink in
And lowly on my face
Start to smile.

Lily Barnes (13)
Simon Langton Girls' Grammar School, Canterbury

The Shadow Monster

I walk through the door
All the lights are off
It's as if I was in a dark, cramped cave
I shout, "Mum!"
No answer

Suddenly the door creaks closed
I turn around, a shiver crawls down my spine
"Hello?"
I hear a small growl and a shadow appears
My heart pounds out of my chest

The shadow creeps through the hallway
It gradually is getting bigger and bigger
I step away with caution
The sound of steps are getting
Quicker and quicker

Slowly a string of spit drops on the floor
The monster shows his fearsome teeth
The shadow leaps like a lion pouncing on prey
I fall to the floor
I am weighed down

I close my eyes
Just then I feel a cold and wet lick drag up my face
The furry beast pins me down
"Bubbles, you frightened me!"

Lucy Watson (13)
Simon Langton Girls' Grammar School, Canterbury

Lost In A Book

When I am bored
I sit on my bed
Wondering where the best book is stored
And set my imagination free in my head

When I open my book
I feel the pages start to shake
I decide to have a closer look
Could it be a mini earthquake?

In a flash I see arms and feet
Golden hair and a scarlet-red hood
What other wonders will I meet?
Maybe a little pig's house made of wood!

They're all dancing on the pages having a blast
The gingerbread man prances with the three blind mice
I shout and I shout, how long will this last?
This book came at a great price!

It was written in the contents
And mentioned in chapter three
Also said in the blurb of its events
And then it dawned on me
My book was alive!
I wish more of my favourite characters will arrive!

Bethan McClean (14)
Simon Langton Girls' Grammar School, Canterbury

Danger, Danger

It's another normal day
And so I come out to play
Rustle, rustle
My mum looks up with fear in her eyes
I can tell she wants me to hide
Danger! Danger!
"Run!" she cries
I am taken by surprise
Thump, thump
In the bushes I cower
My mum standing outside like a tower
Bang, bang
Shots are heard
Out squawks a nearby bird
Silence, silence
There is not a shriek
Or a whistle or a creak
Stomp, stomp
They go away
They carry on with their day
Danger? Danger?
Are you there?
Are you here or anywhere?
Mum! Mum!
There she is!
Why is my stomach starting to fizz?

No! No!
Where is her horn?
I feel too young to even mourn.
Why?
Why?
Oh so now I see
The world has chosen to forget me.

Katherine Lindsay (13)
Simon Langton Girls' Grammar School, Canterbury

Not My Home

The sun is setting
The sky is growing dark
From my spot under the bush
I know it's time to start

My paws sink into the damp grass
I quietly creep across their garden
My whiskers sensing every movement
And my nose is twitching with nerves

I'm conscious they might still be awake
That they could come out any second
But then I think of the prize ahead
And my tummy rumbles in the silent night

The grass changes under my feet
It becomes cold, hard
I lower my back
And push my nose through a plastic flap

Not only does it smell good
It is warm
Comforting
I wish I had a place like this to call home.

I'm creeping over
To a bowl on the floor
I gorge myself
With biscuit heaven!

Leila Duddy (13)
Simon Langton Girls' Grammar School, Canterbury

Way Out

My whole world fell apart
Watching you breaking my heart
I scratch your arm as you're lying there
But all I see is an icy glare

I see the world in shades of monotone
My ears are filling with the sound of a ringing phone
A terrifying scream, a dangerous shout
Sirens blaring as you rush out

The others return, but you're not here
All expressions in the room are of pure fear
I'll miss you every day until the day I die
When you say you're fine, I know it's a lie

I remember the day my heart was broken
I will never forget the words you've spoken
You understand, you believe
That maybe one day we will all be free

One day I hope to see you once more
But until that day, my broken heart will be sore.

Orissa Barrett (12)
Simon Langton Girls' Grammar School, Canterbury

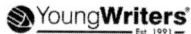

Ghetto Diamond

The rage burns though my veins
Darkness has full control of me
My mind damaged from what I've committed
My tears are dropping inside me

All this terror and conflict
Creates the atmosphere of eternal pain
When has this conflict
Not caused the thunder to empower the waves?

My hopes and dreams
Murdered on this battlefield
Can't they see how dangerous this is?
The old me is dead and gone.

Struggle, quarrel, misunderstandings
Fearing eyes, tightened fits
But there you stand
You shimmer elegantly
You're worth a million lifetimes
You sparkle in the diamond
And who is worthy of all honour
Are we good and evil?
Your last breaths
In that prison
The ghetto.

Maja Dembska (12)
Simon Langton Girls' Grammar School, Canterbury

Black Jacket

Sitting on the roof in my black jacket
We were Romeo and Juliet
Tragic lovers, smoking light cigarettes
Counting down hours, we were showing tattoos
Top of the world, we had nothing to lose
Walking in the rain, in my black jacket
We were Jack and Rose, drowning in the rain
All of my wasted time, for all this pain
Young and free, we were kissing up a hill
All of our lives ahead with time to kill
Lying in your room in my black jacket
We were both falling apart, what to do?
What could I do, what to do now I knew?
Now I was empty and broken-hearted
How could I finish what I had started?
Walking in the rain in my black jacket
What went wrong with you and me?
What went wrong?

Skye Thomson (12)
Simon Langton Girls' Grammar School, Canterbury

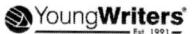

Where On Earth Are They?
Haiku poetry

I'm walking through town
It is raining cats and dogs
Then thunder strikes, *boom!*

I'm waiting at school
My parents yet to be seen
Where on earth are they?

I walk to my house
Hands shaking, door wide open
Where on earth are they?

Trembling I move
My furniture in pieces
Where on earth are they?

Living room in shreds
Pools of blood on the floor
Where on earth are they?

My eyes are teary
I'm shaking, I'm horrified
Here they are, right here

I hear a ticking
I run faster than ever
Throwing myself down

I turn around, *boom!*
I'm back in the street again
I miss my parents.

Lola Hewson (13)
Simon Langton Girls' Grammar School, Canterbury

Death's Hunger

Death
Death is the beast that swallows your soul
It chews you up and swallows you whole
But although we dread it, although we despise it
It must happen to us all

Tonight my time must come to an end
At last I shall join Brahma
Tonight my time must come to an end
And leave the wheel of Samsara

Death steps closer and closer
Pounding at my heart
Death steps closer and closer
It's almost time to depart

Whoosh!
Bang!
I made it through
At last I have joined Brahma

Tonight the stars shine bright and bold
I too shall shine up high
Tonight the stars shine bright and bold
All through the clear dark night.

Duwari Giridharan (12)
Simon Langton Girls' Grammar School, Canterbury

No Reason To Stay

Is there any hope?
I really can't be sure
How? How can we cope?
What is all this for?

Every day they sit
Staring from the surface
They don't really fit
Seem so out of place

And yet they seem plain
Just quite ordinary
But stuck in my brain
Really quite scary

I am not special
A turtle, nothing more
But I am no fool
I know what's in store

I heard fish say 'straws'
'Litter' and 'plastic plates'
I don't know the cause
But I see big mistakes

They appear so empty
Drifting with the waves
They have neither rhyme nor reason
And no permission to stay.

Martha Clegg (12)
Simon Langton Girls' Grammar School, Canterbury

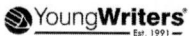

Deserted Darkness
Haiku Poetry

The gunshots echo
Like screams outside my front door
Why can't this just end?

Trudging in the dark
Silence caves in on the town
I have to leave now

No longer tired
I'm shivering to the core
The mud is knee deep

I will be back soon
And with that I said goodbye
For now I'm alone

Shimmering sunlight
I awake under a tree
Sheltered from the rain

The droplets frowning
A rainbow in the distance
No hope left for me

Should I give up yet?
I can't feel my hands - too numb
An abrupt noise sounds

It comes from behind
Shaking the ground in its path
I run like wildfire.

Laila Giles (12)
Simon Langton Girls' Grammar School, Canterbury

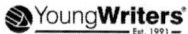

Another Day

The warmness of a hug
The smile on my face
The energy inside me

Then another day

Sitting all alone
Watching the clock tick
Wondering when she'll come home

Waiting, waiting,
Then another day

The clock strikes four
She's finally on her way
I'm warm again and not alone

Then another day
As the sun comes up
Under her pillow
Hoping I'll smile again

Then another day
Waiting, waiting

The clock strikes four
She'll be walking through the door
The clock strikes five

I'm still all alone
The clock strikes seven
She's never coming home.

Emma Deery (12)
Simon Langton Girls' Grammar School, Canterbury

Voices

They come at night
Loud and clear
My head screams as their volume rises
The images they create
Explode in my head
Popping and thumping
The colour of red

They prowl my mind
Searching for weakness
I've built walls to protect myself
But they always fight through
They're getting so loud
I don't know what to do

They scream and shout
They punch and kick
They bend and break
I can do nothing to stop it

This war in my mind
This siege in my brain
Is as cold as winter
I will never feel again

My story is over
My time has come
I say goodbye
While the angels say hi.

Luella-Mai Watson (13)
Simon Langton Girls' Grammar School, Canterbury

Trip To India

My last goodbye to England never came
As the plane took off
I missed everything
Landing was a delight
But my hope to go back home was gone

My mum tried each Indian silk
As did I
But I longed to wear jumpers and denim
My dad tried every curry available
But fish and chips only came to mind

Traditional clothes were vibrant in my closet
As the colours sparkled like glitter
My cousins seemed confused on the different clothes I owned
I challenged myself to try rice and curry
As the taste flourished my mouth

I love India
I will cherish every moment I made here
But how I longed to go back to my home: England.

Tia Anto (12)
Simon Langton Girls' Grammar School, Canterbury

A Sonnet That Would Never Be Sent

The way I feel about you, it scares me
It feels so wrong and yet it feels so right
An emotion deeper than all the seas
In this dark closet, you're my source of light

I want to lie with you and count the stars
If it takes us forever, I don't care
All that's mine I want it to be ours
If I end up in Hell, I belong there

You still don't know, I hope it stays that way
Because I'm just so scared that I'll hurt you
Deep down I know you'll never feel the same
But to know that for sure would hurt me too

I really should accept that you are straight
But just in case you're not, I guess I'll wait.

Iris Hill (14)
Simon Langton Girls' Grammar School, Canterbury

My Home

This is my home
Not a single mobile phone
The red-hot sun
There is no time for fun

Collect plastic bottles
While my little sister toddles
Exchange them for money
For food to fill my tummy

Travel miles for water
Sometimes for an hour and a quarter
Hoping the water will be clean
Endless supply would be a dream

Back at the house
Share a portion fit for a mouse
May have to wait days for more
Have to endure this endless chore

Just last year
We had a massive fear
Had to avoid catching the illness
As medicine is not bill-less

This is my home
Not a single mobile phone.

Claudia Carlotti (13)
Simon Langton Girls' Grammar School, Canterbury

Awaking From Hibernation

A sheet of sparkly snow fresh on the ground
No red berries to be found
Warm brown fur sheltering out the cold
Against the snow my fur is so bold

Freshly-lifted snowdrops scattered all around
Tall trees, white with dappled brown
Icicles dripping as they melt to the ground
Flowing into streams and rivers, making a trickling sound

My thirst is so great
The river is a far too tempting bait
Blinking once, blinking twice
Stretching my arms and legs feels nice

I pull myself out of my den
And finally lumber through the glen
I drink the river water from a glacier
And can not help but be in awe of nature.

Amy Rowland (12)
Simon Langton Girls' Grammar School, Canterbury

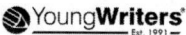

Water

There is a large river between the trees
Which laughs to itself as it runs
It runs through the tall fields of grass
It runs through the city that never sleeps
It runs through the harbour out to sea

Feel the cool liquid between my toes
Feel fresh and cleansed
Feel the rush of the current
To be as swift and strong, oh I wish

The wave covers me like a blanket of blue
The mouth of the ocean swallows me whole
I try to move around the gravity-defying space
Gasping for air
Reaching out for a hand to hold
Can anyone catch me
Take me from the drowning depths
The drowning depths of the ocean.

Isla O'Leary (12)
Simon Langton Girls' Grammar School, Canterbury

Mind Scatter

My mind like a prison
Barricading me from the outside world
I try to move, try to breathe,
But I'm paralysed

Choking on the urge to rid my thoughts
I can't. I won't. I must.
Family, strangers to me
Like seal and sloth

Anxiety engulfs the emotions I didn't know I had
My heart beating slower, slower
A war with my subconscious
And I was losing
Losing what life I had left.

Siberian air tickling my depilated head
The deadpan beats seep into my ear canal
Killing me blind
I knew I was fading, fading,
A second too late
I saw the hospital bed.

Emily Crooks (13)
Simon Langton Girls' Grammar School, Canterbury

Isolated

I hide
Cowering away
This broken shell of a house
A house not a home
Is all I have left in this war zone

Gazing out my window
My only protection
I watch
As the bombs hailing from the sky
Like a snowstorm of death and destruction
I want to get away
What's stopping me?

Sounds of terror and torture fill my ears
I just wish I could escape from this nightmare
I want to get away
What's stopping me?

In the distance I see a lone soldier
Is he heading towards my sanctuary?
Is he coming to save me?
Only time will tell.

Amelia Green (13)
Simon Langton Girls' Grammar School, Canterbury

Can I?

An eerie silence
A blur of white
Snow, dull yet intense
Fixed upon me like cats' eyes

Deep under
I felt myself singing
In a thick cloud of frost
Relentless fear attacked my veins
Can I resist?

Losing control
In a blizzard of emotions
A helpless puppet
At the mercy of my darkest thoughts
Can I find my free spirit?

An attempt to rise
Yet fear drags me down
With its powerful claws
Can I break free?

Breath, hope, light
Elevates my soul
Above my illusion of conflict
Where is my reality?

Athena Martin (12)
Simon Langton Girls' Grammar School, Canterbury

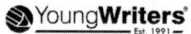

Adolescence

The stage between child and adult
When I'm trying to figure out what I'm about
Sometimes I feel amazing
But others I feel like a fire still blazing
Social media getting me stressed
Nobody's perfect, at least I try my best
Sometimes I wish I was all done growing
But at the moment I'm not sure where I'm going
Lots of choices that are hard to make
Many subjects I want to take
All the homework! I need a break
For time with my friends I'll never make
Sometimes I wish I was a little child,
But my teenage years are worth all the while!

Aoife Mullaney (13)
Simon Langton Girls' Grammar School, Canterbury

Don't Ignore It

It's the first day of school
I was feeling quite cool
But all of a sudden
There was a discussion
About how the world is changing
And how our forests are rearranging
From lots to lost in a short space of time

But the thing I don't get
Is how people just let
This happen
Just pass them
Like it doesn't even matter
Like it's getting any better

But not me
As you will see
I will try to make a difference
For better or for worse
And to listen and to care for
The world we know as
Planet Earth.

Eve Horsfield-Burke (13)
Simon Langton Girls' Grammar School, Canterbury

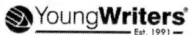

I'm Not A Doggy

I'm not a doggy, I'm a moggy
I'm graceful, calm and purry
I'm not a doggy, I'm a moggy
I'm small, elegant and furry

I'm not a doggy, I'm a moggy
I pounce, I bounce, I land on my feet
I'm not a doggy, I'm a moggy
And I don't howl for a treat

I'm not a doggy, I'm a moggy
I love cuddles, snuggles and strokes
I'm not a doggy, I'm a moggy
And I don't like scruffy coats

You may be confused
Which makes me amused
I'm not a doggy, I'm a moggy.

Anna Murray (13)
Simon Langton Girls' Grammar School, Canterbury

What Does My Pencil Case Think?

Why?
Why do I get used?
Why?
Why do I carry pencils?
Why?
Why do I get put in a big dark bag?
I get shaken around all day
And help do work every day
My home is a dark, dark place
And get carried around at a very fast pace
All my friends are different
But all different colours and styles
I love travelling around school
But I wish I could see the wider world
All of us have the same job
But want to be more to humans
That is our dream and we are all different.

Luisa Williams (12)
Simon Langton Girls' Grammar School, Canterbury

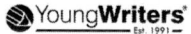

Not Today

I perch on the edge of my bed
Ready to take on the day
The touch of the sun's warming heat
And one breath of the fresh air
Makes anything seem possible...

I jolt up
Rapidly opening my eyes
To the reality of the world

The eerie darkness
Weighing me down
The deathly smell
Stinging my nose
The piercing screams
Haunting my brain
The hate swarming around me
Closing in...

I hold back my pain
I am not giving in
Not today.

Aania Rehman (12)
Simon Langton Girls' Grammar School, Canterbury

Broken Glass

Broken bottles and shattered glass
Trees ripped from their roots
Lakes filled with cement
And crumpled newspaper flung onto gardens

Chemicals, poison and wax sprayed onto our food
Oceans fill up with plastic
Some places engulfed by thick black oil
The sea, once clean
Now suffocating in waste
What has Earth become?

Daily, humans choke from the smoke
Fumes from cars
A broken vision shows a broken future
All in the eyes of a shard of glass.

Marwa Hassan (12)
Simon Langton Girls' Grammar School, Canterbury

Alone

You wake up at the crack of dawn
Against your will
And go, alone

You work all hours
Against your will
And work alone

I clutch the dead bars of this cage
Alone

I see a house in the distance
Three children
Squealing with laughter
They fade
They fade
Like me

I'm alone

But one day
I'll be free from this cage
I'll be free to make my choices
I'll be free from being alone.

Josephine O'Sullivan (13)
Simon Langton Girls' Grammar School, Canterbury

The Devil Of The Wind

Bushes are alight
Australia's on fire
There's no end in sight

What shall we do next?

It's grief, anger, guilt
It's complete devastation
It's utter heartbreak

What shall we do next?

Smoke-filled clouds
Having no power at all
It's all sleepless nights

What shall we do next?

A sun-burned country
The countryside is dying
Waiting for some rain.

What shall we do next?

Summer Hamilton (12)
Simon Langton Girls' Grammar School, Canterbury

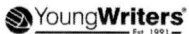

Through The Eyes Of A God

Human lives are so fleeting
Their little hearts barely beating

No knowledge, no power
So weak they sleep hour upon hour

They're oblivious, the fragile insects
Although they have some interesting aspects

They aren't that boring
With their lavish walls and flooring

With many languages and cultures
And funny animals like vultures

The human race isn't so bad
Even if their petty rituals are a little sad.

Annie Boyson (12)
Simon Langton Girls' Grammar School, Canterbury

Roses

You cut me down as a sacrifice
For your overpriced paradise
It honestly amazes me
That you can't see what it's like to be
Assassinated for a day's pretence
For once a year, you play a part
Although your heart is torn apart
The flowers you bring won't make her care
She's well aware that she's being unfair
Don't forget it's all at my expense
I hope everyone here now knows
To think twice before cutting down a rose.

Hannah Oven (13)
Simon Langton Girls' Grammar School, Canterbury

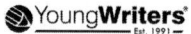

Without A Home

Day after day
People stare and glare
One by one, group by group
I see hundreds of people
People I would like to be
They look at me like a worthless nothing
Why should I deserve a life like this?

Night after night
I curl up in my sleeping bag
And lie down on my concrete bed
Let the long horrifying night begin
Tossing and turning all through the night
I wish I could guess
What life was like not penniless.

Alexa Steadwood (13)
Simon Langton Girls' Grammar School, Canterbury

Hospital

It is so busy
So many people rushing
Some lives are ending
New life entering this world

Hot hospital rooms
Nervous people are waiting
Stuffy waiting rooms
Nurses running urgently

People being cured
Some getting unpleasant news
Unlucky events
Families supporting each other

Exhausted doctors
Long twenty-four hour shifts
Loud ambulances
Make sure every second counts.

Charlotte Rawlins (12)
Simon Langton Girls' Grammar School, Canterbury

Kingfisher

I sit
I spy
Through bramble
An eye
In bushes
They hide
Don't know
That I
Can see them
Fine

Through air
I fly
Red on blue
Sunset on sky
And then
I dive
When I
Arise
A fish
Is mine

A flit
A fleck
A spot
A speck

Six young
Crane necks
The fish
They wreck
For me
Life is
Just one
Long trek.

Elsa Busuttil (13)
Simon Langton Girls' Grammar School, Canterbury

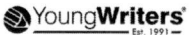

The Red Dog

There once was a dog
But no ordinary one
It was a red dog
Eating a luxury bun

He was near a fair
Lying at the Cornish beach
Lilies in his hair
Eyeing up a yummy peach

He had a noodle
Coming out from the cafe
With a pink poodle
Walking quickly to the bay

There were ice cream trucks
They got a raspberry ripple
And then by pure luck
They found a chocolate triple.

Lily Herron-Jones (12)
Simon Langton Girls' Grammar School, Canterbury

The Crown

This crown shows royalty
It shows marriage, wealth, war and poverty
This crown shows family
It shows love, humour, arguments and disappointment
This crown shows art
It shows colour, scheming, mist and decay
Their crown shows effort
It shows time, sweat, blood and tears
This crown shows time
It shows good, bad, wrong and right
This crown is so much
More than what we think.

Esmé Thompsett (12)
Simon Langton Girls' Grammar School, Canterbury

Flower Field

The crimson flowers in the field
Presenting themselves to the bluebells
Lavender asters blocking with their petal shields
Hoping they don't get thrown down the well
Elegant stunning roses on the other side
As well as the daffodils of gold
They can try to run but they can never hide
They hope they don't get sold
But in the end they are all the same
Just flowers in a field.

Sophie Crane (12)
Simon Langton Girls' Grammar School, Canterbury

Ow! That Hurt!

My eyes are bruised because of you
My hands are swollen because of you
I hardly have any teeth because of you
I lie because of you
I have no friends because of you

Do you care?

I have bad grades because of you
I am scared because of you
I am alone because of you
I am starving because of you
I am an abused child because of you

Do you care?

Miriam Thorpe (12)
Simon Langton Girls' Grammar School, Canterbury

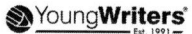

Roses Are Red

Roses are red, violets are blue
I'm not that pretty but look at you
Your eyes, your smile, your light blue hair
Oh how I wish I could stop and stare
You shine so bright you could shade the sun
And when you laugh that's it, I'm done
Roses are red, violets are blue
I hope you like me
As much as I long for you.

Rosie Taborn (13)
Simon Langton Girls' Grammar School, Canterbury

Stop! Stop! Stop!

The clock
Is ticking and ticking
To my inevitable disintegration
If the inconsiderate life
Don't establish their faults
I gasp for air as their waste fills my gills
Along with their grey, deathly smoke
If they do not
Stop stop stop
I will be
No more.

Ella-Mai Rodwell (13)
Simon Langton Girls' Grammar School, Canterbury

I Was His Victim

I see a shadow
A figure
It follows me
Everywhere

After work they are there
At the lamp post
Staring, looking, watching

I'm scared, fearful, frightened
I'm always looking to see
To make sure they are not around

One night, I was walking
Down a gloomy alley
No one was up
No one was around

This figure came behind me
My breath stopped
He whispered, "Elizabeth."

Phoebe Lovidge (14)
Walney School, Walney

Trapped In China

The pain they feel
Is unreal
Locked in animal cages
Like animals

They have been accused
And misused
The sound of begging children
Haunts their ears

Mothers crying rivers of tears
Families look at the barrier wall with fear
Imagine climbing it
Hoping they won't fall

They look up at the dark clouds
Pouring down with rain
Imagining it's their tears after feeling the pain
Wishing they never lived here in the first place
Hoping one day they will find their freedom.

Amna Ramzan (12)
Westborough High School, Dewsbury

The End

The smoke fills the air
With no one to despair
The trees sway for help
Whilst the animals cry and yelp

The black clouds cover the sky
Friends and family watch up high
They know this would be their last goodbye

So let's all stand together
All we need is some cold weather
Never mind, it's too late
Time to pack up and evacuate.

Libby Williams (14)
Westborough High School, Dewsbury

Aerial Adventure

And there it was, everything that mattered to me,
A beautiful, delicate, woven tapestry
Of fair fields and beauteous buildings; a view
That only those who fully experienced it knew
Was inexplicable for its wondrous escapade.
And from this adventure are memories that stayed.

Every home was like an autumn leaf lying gently
On the Earth, and around them was consequently
The green of the trees, and the roads shining like silvery
Stems on a frosted morning. The clouds were witchery-
They were puffs of pure white magic in acres of blue.
Yet, why at times do they cry with fierce, sonorous thunder too?

This is what I saw but let me tell you how I felt:
The exhilarating feeling and fresh air that I smelt,
The wonderful lights that stole my breath away,
Just to breathe the sweet air was better than a parfait!
My rejoicement poured out me like sunshine through
A transparent window; I glowed from inside too.

Unfortunately, all good things come to an end;
And as the ground grew ever closer, I descend,
Enjoying every last memorable moment, and
While devastated that I am about to land,
Briefly go over my incredible venture,
Which I will forever remember - my aerial adventure.

Rowan Abass (13)
Wirral Grammar School For Girls, Bebington

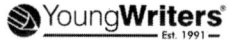

YOUNG WRITERS INFORMATION

We hope you have enjoyed reading this book – and that you will continue to in the coming years.

If you're a young writer who enjoys reading and creative writing, or the parent of an enthusiastic poet or story writer, do visit our website **www.youngwriters.co.uk**. Here you will find free competitions, workshops and games, as well as recommended reads, a poetry glossary and our blog. There's lots to keep budding writers motivated to write!

If you would like to order further copies of this book, or any of our other titles, then please give us a call or order via your online account.

Young Writers
Remus House
Coltsfoot Drive
Peterborough
PE2 9BF
(01733) 890066
info@youngwriters.co.uk

Join in the conversation!
Tips, news, giveaways and much more!